The Bride of E

Books by Mary Jo Bang

The Bride of E
Elegy
The Eye Like a Strange Balloon
Louise in Love
The Downstream Extremity of the Isle of Swans
Apology for Want

The Bride of E

Poems

Mary Jo Bang

Graywolf Press

Publication of this volume is made possible in part by a grant provided by the Minnesota State Arts Board, through an appropriation by the Minnesota State Legislature; a grant from the Wells Fargo Foundation Minnesota; and a grant from the National Endowment for the Arts, which believes that a great nation deserves great art. Significant support has also been provided by the Bush Foundation; Target; the McKnight Foundation; and other generous contributions from foundations, corporations, and individuals. To these organizations and individuals we offer our heartfelt thanks.

Published by Graywolf Press
250 Third Avenue North, Suite 600
Minneapolis, Minnesota 55401
All rights reserved.

www.graywolfpress.org

Published in the United States of America

Printed in Canada

ISBN 978-1-55597-539-5

2 4 6 8 9 7 5 3 1
First Graywolf Printing, 2009

Library of Congress Control Number: 2009926850

Cover design: Kyle G. Hunter

Cover art: David Levinthal, *Café*. Courtesy of Exposure NY.

Contents

PART II

for Mark Bibbins

PART I

ABC PLUS E: COSMIC ALONENESS IS THE BRIDE OF EXISTENCE

A pack of young flirts was patrolling the party,
They were cultural outsiders, consumed with . . . what?
Their own notion of beauty as reflected in the shine-more mirror
Of a man's pants? Or nothing
But midnight and no one is counting.

They were practitioners, they admitted to the barman,
Of psychological materialism, explaining they had read both
Sartre and de Beauvoir and believed in the cerebellum,
The thalamus and the lower brain and that between
The lower and the upper parts there must be room for them,
Néant [nothingness] aside.

Indeed, the evening was a spectacular bacchanalia,
The girls lugging their blind-drunk partners around the floor.
One sitting it out with a volume of *The Collected Camus,*
That one was "imperious" (the word is de Beauvoir's).
"The club was plunged into almost total darkness,
With violinists wandering about
'Playing soulful Russian music' into the guests' ears."
"'If only it were possible to tell the truth,'
Exclaimed Camus at one point."

There was vodka and champagne, both in quantities
Extremely beautiful and nice for getting tight. And dancing
Cheek to cheek, between the exchange of furtive kisses
And giggles every time one of the chaps said, "Don't
Leave me, I love you, I'll always love you."
Which they took as irrefutable evidence
Of a general greed for human warmth,
I.e., for touch, even among the agonized
Post-adolescent dreamers who morphed on the dance floor
That night into naughty boys, echoing the girls' questions
Of "how shall we live," "what shall we do,"
Words without end, without weight.

A EQUALS ALL OF A SUDDEN

At work one night
A truck driver had a truck
All of a sudden.
On the second shift, I spoke up:
"How would it be if." "Go ahead."
I took. I borrowed. I turned.
I knew. And from then on
I was the anything that wanted done.
Maybe. Because of.
In between times I went.
All in all things were very bad.
As for me, I was still thinking, why not?
The longer I thought,
The more determined I became.
Up to this time, I had been in a boat.
Why boats?
Homeric. A small fishing box. A toolbox
To support purgatory.
All of a sudden, I was still working.
To leave early I packed a few things,
Set my alarm, went to bed.
I decided to postpone.
I wanted to go back.
I drove back.
I didn't go in as the water was awful.
I felt. I drove. I stopped. I started betting.
I was really lucky for a change.
Then I started getting unlucky.
I lost a lot of valuable time.
I went home. Bed was the highway
That suited me in a bad rain.
The next day. One day. On the 16th
Around 12:30 p.m.
I had a thought:
The days were going by

Certainly. I had a fact: 29.
1660. 1/3. 5 years. Death.
I began thinking, I don't care.
Did you notice?
I worked with things in general.
One evening I came into work
And asked the maintenance men
If I was in the same category
As sweeping up trash off the floor.
The foreman said, "I want a pass."
He looked directly at me.
I could see his eyes
Boring straight into me.
Then I went home
And wrote up a script
To follow where I got a free boat ride
While taking pictures of pictures
And all the pictures came out beautiful.
I began thinking
About thought more.
14 hours a day.
The year was coming to a close.
All of a sudden I was looking
For the next day. It was just time,
I decided, a day. Shine down on me,
I told the four-calendar café,
And on your own square floor.
It was dark all of a sudden
And I translated that
Into a foreign text
That would see me through
Every subsequent day:
"In the dark we played capture the flag."
No, not in the dark but in the all
Of a sudden lacerating absence.

AND AS IN ALICE

Alice cannot be in the poem, she says, because
She's only a metaphor for childhood
And a poem is a metaphor already
So we'd only have a metaphor

Inside a metaphor. Do you see?
They all nod. They see. Except for the girl
With her head in the rabbit hole. From this vantage,
Her bum looks like the flattened backside

Of a black-and-white panda. She actually has one
In the crook of her arm.
Of course it's stuffed and not living.
Who would dare hold a real bear so near the outer ear?

She's wondering what possible harm might come to her
If she fell all the way down the dark she's looking through.
Would strange creatures sing songs
Where odd syllables came to a sibilant end at the end.

Perhaps the sounds would be a form of light hissing.
Like when a walrus blows air
Through two fractured front teeth. Perhaps it would
Take the form of a snake. But if a snake, it would need a tree.

Could she grow one from seed? Could one make a cat?
Make it sit on a branch and fade away again
The moment you told it that the rude noise it was hearing
          was rational thought
With an axe beating on the forest door.

B IS FOR BECKETT

There is so little to say.

BEAST BRUTALITY

The caption read,
"He and she standing quietly next to a dog."

The prompt queen sat with her crown on,
The insets between each Gothic arch providing a measure

Of what can be
Done with architecture.

She said, "We built it long ago.
And then we knocked it down."

And then she looked away.
"And then we looked away."

C IS FOR CHER

Culture miniature and clad as Cleopatra, she descends
A set of semicircular steps
Tiled in a geometric mosaic pattern

And there she finds the answer: everything
Changes depending on whether
You're up or down. Behind her,

A high-relief rectangle proscenium,
Beside her, whatever intrigued her last.
An unofficial fan leaps feverishly into action. At that,

She seems to multiply. History will be filled
With the shower of dots that will become her.
At that, she becomes. It's complex.

Through the glass she sees a pair of dazzling slippers.
At dinner her drink was called a Vladimir,
Hers was the plate that contained Washington oysters.

There she held a fork. There she was on a stage
Of discourse. Of course. Mickey Mouse comes over
And stops to stare. Cher is dressed in a long gold dress.

The sequins form stripes. "If I could turn back time."
She's singing. And Mickey in his red pants is acting
Like the goodwill minister to an enraptured world.

Mickey thinks. He turns the corner.
To the gift shop: ever open.
He buys retractable mother-of-pearl opera glasses

As a present. Yes, it's over. The present.
In which you discovered forward-thinking thought.

CAT'S CRADLE, COMMA THIS

The note rises from something awful.
A woman in a jam. Train wreck of crumpled cars.
Toppled causes. An hour composed

Of: Look at that how
The hand stutters as it cuts the pie.
A second stands and is then annihilated.

The string taut, a trip taken
Across some empty center.
The Grand Canyon. A metal ladder

She climbed down. Her sister somewhere
To this. A striking continuity. The tripwire
Tripped again. The second time

The trap sprung shut. We are nothing left of this
Except this. Afterwards,
The battle scenes preoccupy.

The engagements now absurd.
The fighting figures erased
By the comic-book clash between forces

Malevolent and miraculous.
Dynamic migration of sunlight across the slats
That form the floor.

The photograph of it finally making it strange
Enough to see ourselves in it.
You over there in the half black we call gray.

Me in the white that wears nothing more.
Torso. Arms gone. Translation
Becomes adaptation. Each face a doll's

Face. Manikin back. The cake on the plate
Becomes a piece of the party.
A panda-face balloon held in suspension

By helium. A doctor in a white coat plays
The scientist who dismantles the dummy; he says,
Look at the ectoplasm under the cover plate.

Look at the interlocular spaces.
Look at a man's hat. It becomes
A stringless kite. Now it falls asleep. Now

It gets up. The white coat glows in the dark
Until it becomes the light of the emphatic
Filament. This will not let you go.

CONSIDER THIS CORRUPTION

In the film concerning the cult of the living,
The woman was taken.
Some people looked at her and said nothing
And some said one interpretation is that

All action is in the mind, a cluster of notions
In depravity's head independent of the dreadful
Invention of the magnetic temporary where
A partition is positioned between right and wrong.

On the back of the partition,
On the aspect from which she and we are reading,
It is written: Everyone is reckless sometime.
What will come next? There is no worse punishment

Is there than this other empty body:
       The eyes half-closed, the canvas in back
whitewashed into a steady gaze. We are appalled
apparently. We are held up by a rug-covered table.

The gift is the effortless image of bent rebar lengths
Encircling a neck. Thank you.
We are for all intents and purposes broken.

D IS DYING, AS ONE GOING IN THE DARK

A feeling of something indefinable but not right.
Not comfortable. A rushing.
Sometimes I have to stop
And sort out time at cyberspeed.

It's supposed to arrive "between 2 and 3 in the morning."
The very specificity of the promise makes me disbelieve.
If it ever arrives, I'll say, Good, that's over.
That little irritating suspense.

The hollowing wait. The stupid want
For good news. No bad. What more can one ask for?
One day more over in the prison
Of childhood. The runaway fantasies.

The retreat into the open mind,
That mysterious conceptual nothing.
Distant fireworks. Boomph, boomph, boomph.
Someone left the cake out in the rain. MacArthur Park.

A half-moon with a mottled veil over it.
The hum of childhood politeness.
"Do you remember me?"
He said, "Yes, church." I said, "That's right,"

And kissed his cheek. His gray beard felt so soft.
An engine keeps making the noise of an interior radio
Through which I hear a machine that keeps churning
Out: "For I seem dying,

as one going in the dark / To fight a giant—."
All the petty errors of life.
Let's take that wiring apart and see how it works.
Like that. As if it could be done.

DEATH AND DISAPPEARANCE

A plague. The population shaped by the spread.
The meeting with mammals whose bones are not found
Upright anymore. The slow pandemic and its subsequent
Effect. The unusually high rate of devastation.

Winter and spring. Take any year and it's possible to infer
The purple spots on abdomen or limbs.
The overwhelming priority. The impoverishment with
Every outbreak. The corpses in recurrent waves.

A pyre burning the molecular biology
Of the virulent strain and taking with it the haunting evocation
Of a face. A cluster of cases provides whatever
With no knowledge of exactly how. With no possible

Undermining flowering of certainty. The dark outsider status
Of the mechanical animal. Gear churn. Lung bellow.
A foot thumping in the rib cage. Back and forth.
The limited skills for finding what can no longer be seen.

Only a surround where one feels seriously cheated.
As if beat handily. As if exploited. As if a wide variety of poses
That resemble manikins. The fascinating nature of
The stratagems of staggering forward with exhaustion

Into the final further line of inquiry.
The body becoming meat and bone and the iconographic
Culture saturated with reaction. The subject itself
Now manifested in any number of ways as a formless arc.

Swaddled in the basic fact of layers of purpose
That simply become profoundly brutal. The aura escaping
Description except as an empire of trouble where cells line up
To meet the edge where the car takes the body away.

E IS EVERYWHERE

A blackout occurs and then we return to routine:
The inhumane blather on the screen.
The light glares in, illuminating each shadow.
"Do you feel it?" "Those sad mysteries?"

The bells are ringing, indicating
An original longing has been transformed
Into a pitch too high to hear.
Now an unsettling magician's girl comes on stage

And plays herself. It is all very "upsetting"—
In Freudian terms. This vague echo
Of something unnamed.
This ruefully apocalyptic drama

Where the I is thrust into the Darwinian claw.
And now a bird, overheard, realizes its dream of flying.
Beneath it, the bridge, a passage
From contemplation hidden in a classic

"Love me?" Yes, he loves her. Lastly,
There is the redemptive conceit
That links the transfiguration journey
With this pomp, this sequence, this wedding

Of the eyes with their lens of miraculous glass.
The eyes that see the emphatic "Hey,
Teacher, leave those kids alone."
The crowd shouts the lyrics back to the band.

And now, someone is saying, "It's amazing
That an Australian platypus is now a curio
On a shelf in a cabinet in a palace in Poland."
All the while, you're wondering

About the man on the curb who waved at you.
As if he knew you.
As if you have been everywhere. As if you are existence.

THE ELECTRIC EVENTUAL

Someone snaps and suddenly shatters the static abstract.
Dates get strung along string.
Convoluted stories become stories
After the facts are condensed. Something like this:
You asked for it. You got yourself born in a hospital bed
And now there's no going back.
Except to see sheep in fog. Sheep in fog.
It's all you see. Gray shapes fading
Into a larger gray form. Day shutting its windows.
Blackout fabric on the bed where you toast
Between the sheets.
The simple ideal that you set for yourself:
No endless self-adding whitewashed winter.
A purple blue-black sky is the uniform overhead sight.
Gray dust on the dresser, white on the side
Of a digit drawn along the surface
Of the leaf next to the thorn. And cold now.
Cheeks flushed, a flipping banter fluttering
In the brain. In the background, an exclamation mark.
In the black habitat of nightfall, from the eave is the icicle.
That drip-drip-drip, a ridiculous spectacle.
Inside the house, near the proximal banister—
A thing of significance: death with a name on a bracelet.

F IS FOR FORGETTING

How complicated is it? How are you?
Thank you too. And with this, forward we go.
There is so little part of forgetting
That makes up the total—a silver image

Of a boat on water sits and sits.
Time ago is then. Now time
To look at the dummy
At the table, his head slumped over

His cereal bowl. Look at him. He's on a stage.
He is silently sizing up the table he takes in
As he stares down. This is the world
When it's reduced down to a moment.

The mind doesn't halt but goes halfway up
In the elevator and then finds itself stuck.
This is the entirety. Eternity. Made of a material
That is unlikely to change but is forever.

Even when the eyes are closed they see
The barricade. At the edge of a cliff is a brink.
The sky is the color of blue.
Blue is on all the closed windows.

Inside, the dummy's face disappears into the hole
Of his bowl. Behind him, there's the cryptic
Schematic master plan
Where the surrender is redacted.

FOR FREUD

I didn't mean to imply a girl is nothing
More than a jewel box.
They keep misreading me. Imagine
The rough brush of the horsehair chair,

The soft brush of wanting
To rescue reason from dizziness, some cue,
The tempting answer to, 'What shall I do?
What shall I be of?' The lower rank

Of the snapshot as compared to
The print in the frame.
A milder feeling hovers over me. I'm dead,
Liebchen. What does it matter, that

The Great Wall of China has become an example
Of middle-period capitalism in action?
Think Carthage. Think of the strange
New Mexico spaceship some people say they've seen.

Saucer disk. Anna, kiss me. She won't
Stop mourning. There is seldom but sometimes
That sort of love. Where the one in the chair
At the end puts on your greatcoat and cries.

FOR THE FINAL REPORT

Final Report: The 13th. No progress
Until 10 July.
Tuesday is worried.
Today didn't come back
Again until 2 or 3.
Still trying to sort out the morning yesterday.
The day and all evening
A terrible headache. Back to bedtime.
Still working on revisions
To the Napoleon machine.
It keeps churning out the question of how
Can I wait and see how I feel.

I woke up and couldn't convince myself
To work on 2/3. Why is this happening?
I slept. But I'm hoping for more from the gray one.
I really wonder whether all is going on
In so many words. I have to tell someone
At 3 to sleep. I don't need much.
A pin under a nail. Either way.
It seems a bit tangential to something
Of an explanation.

Back pain until mid-September.
I don't know.
If I did, I would take that wiring apart
And see how it works. Like that.
As if it could be done. He wondered if I would . . .
What? Whatever it is of course I'll do it.
I have to remind myself
That it makes no sense to be crushed.

Chalk and crayon face, tree trunk the shore
Of the social sphere that turns and turns and turns.
I keep my eyes closed
At the verge of a chasm.
A space-heater rumination.
That thing that is buried.
You believe in it
Because you've been told it is there.
It's not a bad feeling.
I do not think it will.

GHOST AND GRAYS

The women were possessed.
Smiling in an understated manner
That is characteristic of those who sit on sofas.
Who draw them up in front of the frequent spectacle
Of men playing cards with machine guns
On the floor next to them. One guy

In a pastel armchair, an obstinate idealized peach,
Asleep to the eye, but not for nothing was he there.
To keep the peace. To answer a question.
If you touched his arm lightly
His potentially expressive eyes would open
To both renounce sleep, and to announce

A head and hand willingness to flee the region
To get whatever it was you wanted—
If he could have it. Something
For the mercurial stomach? Something to bathe with
That would turn the water an aqua blue.
He too was sly. And now he was waiting impassively

For the question that was about to be posed.
And she was looking absent-mindedly
Around as if a need has suddenly presented itself.
What was there to know, was what she was wondering.
The old error of thinking, the navigation of a globe
Of honesty traded for the latest

And not-yet famous ghost of one's own ruin.
And what precaution could be taken? Something
Separated two moments. Something became a coast
Against which she passed along staring
Into the difference between.

H IS HERE IS A SONG, NOW SING

The clouds above are speaking
But what they say doesn't mean much.
So be it. It's the end
Of a choir and now you've divided yourself
From yourself. Now you're something simple.
You know there's an answer for everything
But you can't find one for nothing-to-do.
You wait and you wait.
You learned this from watching the oncoming
Drag behind it one gray burial train.
As in, "One stands alone."
It's a permanence persisting.
Picture yourself in the now as one on an iceberg,
There since the beginning.
It's all you know. The sequential
Where consequence follows an action.
Where the ear hears you singing: Nirvana
Over easy. An icicle traces a statement
On the mellowed snow: "It's a terrible moment."
The goblet mouth on the table speaks
To your thirst, saying, "Longing, your longing, is infinite."

HER IN THE EYE OF A HURRICANE

This: a woman lazing on a chaise longue.
Someone is speaking to her.
Nothing wrong.
Nothing more right
Than a storm brewing in the green park.

While to one side, Clark is looking
At Lois Lane's legs
As they sit face to face with rope or tape
Binding their feet to the floor
And wrists to the chair.

"Do you love me, Bunny," one says
To the other. "I love you," Bunny says.

The story's dedication hidden—
In the lavender-red of a chair's ruffled edge
On the splash page—
Is where we leave the story. Hurricane? Or hope?
Why not? It's the little difference between.
In all there's a formal extravagance.

The subject is the finger on the shutter button.
The proscenium arch recedes as Hamlet asks,
"What is going on?" Now
We're in the play. Hamlet turns his back
And the arch comes back,
Breaking up a frame. The surface is a notion.

A measured revealing. "Now
I see," she says to Clark.
Seeing was no longer perceiving.
The picture is complicated.
The clouds obscure the weather vane.
The woman walks to the edge.

Waves crash against a background
That is a curatorial choosing culminating in a set
Of black-and-white images
Of tree branch, tree branch, tree branch.

And yet, our subject, the figure, a woman, recedes
Into the art of adoration where someone
Keeps thinking repeatedly, I'll love you endlessly.

She slips her hands from the rope.
Vastness was like a sea. In the center, a seam.
Of course, there was also the future.
Now she moved further away

Which was also where the mob was moving
Along the sidewalk. The white wall barricade.
Awful was what was being said, over and over:
In the sea inside her mind, there was a picture

Of a dragon threading itself around a giant
Ship. The green of snake green.
Of parrot green. Of grass green. Emerald
Green mixed with blue at the edge

Where liquid met the last white marks on the gray
Rock. They were evidence of recurrence.
A sun, some light, a length of rope, a painting
Called *The Dream*. Yes,

The sea of the present kept meeting
The vast. The sun. "The insomnia
That had haunted the night.
In the heart, fear settled into a soothing rub-dub,

Rub-dub. Like men in a tub look back
On the deep they've just escaped—
The aqua bottom of the pool
Tinting the water blue—to wish

The boat oars on the plastic raft had been easier,
My mind a top stopped, looked back
And woke. In a place no one had been
And went back."—Dante

I AS IN JUSTICE

Just this: Consider that you are here and there
Is a bar or six at the window and you are dying
To escape. And on the television
The operatic

Which is sometimes called the nightly news.
In between cuts of carnage, the click
Catches and claims the marzipan
Blue behind it. A hand unzips the blue,

And reaches through and strokes the cat,
Calico, old, and tending to fat.
You know this thin scene
Is lit by the heedless light at the end

Of a harrowed day. Curiosity and hunger
Give rise to wanderlust. Then back
To the program: "If you look at the brain . . ."
Not everyone agrees but it's clear

There is an immense power in uncertainty.
There is that story that goes like this:
You were a crime you didn't know had been committed.
And it's that not knowing, the sine qua non

Of uncertainty, that holds the person in
Place. I can't tell you how to think
Of it but for some it's seen
As an overambitious stranglehold.

Think garrote at the neck. And then think
Of how silly it sounds
To say afterwards, "I was angry,"
When what you might have said was,

"Surely what I wish for you can't be worse
Than what fate has in store."

I IN A WAR

With waking. The racing mind slides
Into the fog of morning, the river's far flank barely visible.
A taut classic elastic band vibrates across the sand dune
Of history. Private and public. Plastic

The burial outfit, black over bland and wearable.
The fright is only half-felt
When you see the photos of death as a bear rug.
A come-see-me look. Here's another: Death serving tea

In a twee room with no windows
But still trompe l'oeil sills
And swagged curtains with tiebacks
Á la the kitsch of some vague Versailles.

And now forward, into the fog, driving a golf cart,
A tear in the corner of your eye produced
In spite of the ironically undercut temple of truth.
"Ruth," he said, and she opened the bible and found herself

Looking up at a televised picture
Of three stooges. Here's an eye: let us poke it.
Here's an ear: let us twist it. Neither was satisfying.
Neither told the whole story. Some between

What could be seen and what couldn't was a Grand Canyon
Cut by water and submerged seven times in the history
Of keeping a record by testing rock via carbon dating.
Religion played no role in that rain.

In that wearing away at the idea of the hidden.
And what was hidden but the bottom?
Green and Edenic. The barest beginning.
A predictable ending waiting for warring factions,

Infractions of mutuality. A riot wishing for a cause
That was worth it. Fire and razor wire wrapping.
Fanaticism projecting itself
Onto the blank screen of The Other. Of course there's I

Understand that I'm not alone. I'm only asking
That you see the morning for what it is. A lamentation
For the sentient state.
The mocking sign that says, "Day transforms

The vapor to the nada the eye can see."
The burial outfit laid on the bed of last night.
Some darling boy acting like a mirror-bearing acolyte,
Hitting the high notes in the darkest dawning.

You know the moment: the eye forming the catalyst
That causes the coincident moment of recall.

JUST SEEN, JUST SAID

The air of mystery. The sense of mystery
By virtue of the fact of the speaker's gaze
That seems to come from a significant remove
From the subject—

In a Robbe-Grillet novel, *La Jalousie,*
A man spends his days watching his beloved from behind the blinds
And the window.

The innocent eye records
To the point where a subject like the truth is obliterated.

In spite of that the speaker admits that
Inherent in the descriptive is the act or instance of resigning.

The jetty will be submerged. "Riveted to some detail
Of the desert—."
On the path there were wrecked cars

Set in scenes of the contemporary
World. They augmented the list of timeless dangers.

"This is what I was before—"
The brain cool in the water.
The door closed against the instant.

K AS IN F BLANK BLANK K

The friction. The fire. Without the breathless wonder
In front of you. The swimming suit,
The sand.

The book on the nightstand.
In the old way. Open the book.
Here's one beginning: the crab dragged its claws

Across the desert. Sad as sobbing. Sad as what
Our half feet felt as we crawled
From the shallow sea-salt water.

Here's another: Krazy Kat watches while Alice falls
Headfirst and catches a forward jar
Of marmalade in the dark.

Someone whispers, "You
Are surrounded by evil."
Then, "Christ,

Look at the way you use language here
In the common area." And believe me, I know.
Look away, look again.

At that, we can see
The art of the act of the moon
And the earth matching up on the plasma screen.

L EQUALS LOOK

At a book of details
Of all the moments when knowledge is acquired.

A sort of expanded balloon
Sighs and says, "We are what came before."

"The storm in the window of the mind,"
The sleeping sister says while she's walking around

Wonderland watching
A cat touching down and talking.

Not a car in sight. A cemetery seen from the air.
All the obelisks you could ever ask for.

M AS IN MASKS

The psychic investiture of a seal, an impression
Badly done of some other who presented
One morning as a caricature
Of a crying doll in a cradle with Freud leaning over
A mirror and seeing only the bottom of his beard.
Why do we? And one day not
Yet or not always or not ever?
The body as document burning in an ashtray,
The scene in front changing, a flipbook
Feeling the current in front on it.
Ions on a sofa, a sanguine moment at thirty
Of and after. A document: sturdy, unpatented, private
Prosthesis, partly dispatched
Into a pocket. Add a structure of obligation, a cultural
Ditto. Unstable signifier. The wearer is something
The feel of fabric behind which is the one I; the one
Gnawing a nail while looking up—
At the white trim that is winter white
While against it the dark behind the mask
Imparts a sense of intimacy
In the moment and expands to fill the frame.

MAGIC MAKES EVERYTHING RIGHT

A bite tastes like an incidental pleasure
Without the risk of backfire, a knife
From the nine-truck convoy driving out of a nine-circle hell.
"What's the hurry?" "Siege state."

There is no more.
There was the normal black bowler hat.
There was a rabbit.
A long scarf kept coming out of the cuff of a coat.

The end was then stuffed into a magician's mouth.
"He might be a ventriloquist's doll," an assistant was saying.
Behind the scarf was Jerry Mo's face.
The stage curtain hung behind it.

All this at the end
Of a thumb-sucking sort of day where no had echoed
Through the cosmos and the axe in the back
Of a head meant brutality was all around you.

Muffled by the leafing of pages
[The sound. The sound. The sound.]
Through the bookshelf: The caption at the bottom of the page read,
"He and she standing quietly next to a dog."

Of course. The prompt queen sat with her crown on.
The viewer could see the empty insets between each Gothic arch.
They provided a measure of what was right.

MYSTERY AT MANOR CLOSE

—Quickly Brenda stepped aside and tripped up the Biology Mistress.

She puts her ticking wrist to her ear and hears a house
Full of *Tock* from the clock that is lacking a stem.
On the face it says Mickey and Mouse.
(All of which comes from within.)

She makes a wish: that the Heather who left her
In stormy weather will find herself
In the mire of desires that cannot be easily realized.
To your health, she says, and sticks out her foot

To feel the fire in its place. Here's to Bio-
In most of its many spheres. To the ear that hears
The clack of a gate latch. To the mouth and its legible
Little gray lies. To the brain with its hardwired fear.

And to cathexis, both far or near. Back at the manor,
There's mystery: a van and a driver, a girl's guide, a book.
The rescue of one in a basket about to be driven away by a crook.
The Freud finger puppet appears on stage and says, in German,

"Yes, Liebchen, it's true.
We are born to begin and to end
In infantile fury."
The girl on the couch, who is listening, doesn't say a word.

N AS IN NEVERMORE

The raven is stuffed now
Into the shape of a principal
Taxidermic moment. The snapshot shows it

As it was when it was alive and staring
Down from the doorframe
And onto what we are when all but defeated.

"To define is to make material," so says the raven—
Below it is the eerie highway
Known as an ever-death.

Ravaged by war and war's enigmatic attacks
By a rocket constructed of parts
And blended into an incendiary whole.

One way to see the bird is to look at it
As a fragment of violence mixing its message
With the cold roar of constant utterance.

Quoth the raven, "Give me more—."
Mis- means mistake as in shell-game catastrophe.
The arm is a line that points to the start.

A bar or six at the window and dying
Again. And on the small screen
The bird turns back into the whining operatic.

Into the story of key elements:
Accident and design with an ending
That ties up the plot rather nicely.

Although outside the box there is mockery spilling over
Onto the unwitting wish: to be and to be and to be
Better. And over that, love's layer of happy shellac.

"Only when I'm posing do I feel real,"
This from the invisible crowd, this
From the death's head. This from the bird

Looking down on a square where
A woman is brushing back her hair.
Her name is Lenore Nevermore.

NIGHT AFTER NIGHT

There it is, night after night: the street
With its zebra crossing.
The lake with its lights. The insect ferry.
The map overlay. Is this a vein?
Is this an artery? Is this the opening

Out of which the liquid spills
Onto the surgical table?
A pane of green glass watches
While a white sheet turns red.
The heart empties itself. It used to be

An engine. Now, it's a twice. Morning is
One, night is two. Three is what will be.
The rat is under the kitchen counter.
The cupboard is bare.
Me, me, me, I don't care.

O IS IN OUTSIDE

Outside is the pastoral aspect: the green, the stream.
We stepped on a rock. On a jagged slab of concrete pavement
Thrown there. How? When? The water broke against the edge.
A soap-suds billowed up. Why? Sink water

And laundry residue. So, not a stream. Not a rock.
A waste ditch deep and wide enough
To seem like a landscape with a slab of broken concrete.
Domestic porcelain fixture. Cosmetic veneer.

The kitchen sink. Place towels I-beam to I-beam.
Make a chamber. The sleeping smell of the slanted hill.
The worried sound of inside, the clarity of the forceful eye.
The ear. The rain. Beginning to drive.

The green elbow. Repeating symptoms: fever, chills.
Surgery. Now, the green elbow scars instead.
What did you say? Yes, the scar fills in for perfection.
For the quotidian cardinal male red who said.

The church at the bottom of the hill.
The white vestments of the priest at the door.
Goodbye to the flock. The funnies.
The Beetle Bailey green uniforms. The uncle.

The khaki. The uniform hill slope.
The propensity for fever. The fever pitch of the hill.
The scar formed from a box.
Of course outside leads in. I never said it didn't.

I'm living, aren't I. Bleeding from the elbow.
That won't heal. For my shoe I cut cardboard
Every morning. The shape of the heel. Fine,
Outside is also out. In the shadows. The prison of.

Runaway fantasies. The march in the courtyard.
The open mind wandering dazed around.
A baby crying a background.
Eternal imagined judgment.

Terror of being. That mysterious conceptual nothing.
A worn electrical wire connects all the lights.
They go and you say, Good,
That little irritating suspense is over.

The hollowing wait. The stupid puncture of rejection
That, in the moment, wears a human face.
A scowl oftener and oftener.
Chrysanthemums color, the larger new

Swallowing the previous smaller ones.
Boomph, boomph, boomph. MacArthur Park.
Someone left the cake out in the rain.
A surreal film in black and white.

On and off the interior radio through
Which a pin is under a nail.
Or you don't know what that's like?
Either way. (Let's take that wiring apart

And see how it works. Like that.
As if it could be done.) It's such a distance
To move across the green grass expanse.
Walking, is it better to keep the eyes closed

Or open to an assailant sand-grate in the psyche?
The four-story inventory mocks, "I had the common
Experiences plus the less. Listen, how common is that?"
After the fall. The terrible empty room.

She said yes and turned.
Outside was outside.
The eternal didn't exist in this lifetime.
"Trust me," she said. On the wall was a painting.
Behind it a wall and a hook.
On the surface was the surface.
"Listen to me," she said. And he listened.
Started and stopped. Holding onto a handrail
The wood warm from the radiators on all sides.
"Yes," she said, and turned to the phone.
Feeling the feel of what begins with
The sound of a cat. The sound of a car.
A soup bowl not empty, not full.
"The difference is what I've omitted," she said,
"In a listing of the acts of cruelty that exceed the quotidian."
She said yes and turned to the painting.
"Listen to me," she said.
Trees coming in the window.
Some salve on a scar.
Some racket of the sounds that enter and exit the head.
She thought she could feel the impulse of her pulse.
But only for a second. Then she was back in the exterior.
Facing the form of four presidents.
Some sunglasses cutting the light down.
A dog with a muzzle moving toward a wall.
She slammed the car door.
The trees matched the window.
She looked into the mirror and saw herself turning
Into a movie viewer looking at a cliff face.
The lights going up at the end. "Isn't it lovely,"
Says Annie to Sandy, as she looks and sees something.
Listen to the soundtrack later
Feeding the dog a spoonful of medicine.
Polishing a shoe. "In real life be careful," she said,

"Of the collective guile." But here, in the well,
Just listen and sleep in the world beyond this one
Where there is a stage and a stack of playbills
And a sand dune and a woman who turns now and then
To speak to a man out of sight.
It's the end and it isn't. I love you except when I don't.
You get some doll furniture to make a set. To see how to act.
How to build a backdrop of the faceless coming over
The never have I seen so many. I didn't know.

OUTNUMBERED AT 0

The pictured environment: an anchor tattoo
In amber, and a cold face
like an equally icy chandelier at the top

Of the cage. It's April again. It's October.
That's what I said.
It's over, like a ghost in the going to go,

Okay, here's the door. See
The trim around the rectangle.
Let's walk around,

Get closer to the center. Come over here, sister. Line up
For the photo. It's August.
You have on sunglasses. It's February.

It's snowing. I know
It keeps changing.
You're wearing a jacket.

You're going, Okay, here's the door. See the trim
Around the rectangle. Walking around
Getting closer to the center. The forecast:

No rain and yet you're dead center
Of an eddy.
Listen, we interfere with our own wrath

From the completely unknown
Inside of a cardboard horse.
I.e., objectivity is overestimated.

P EQUALS PIE

Let's place Plato on one side.
Let's place Pee-wee Herman on the other.
It's worth noting the Greek root, techno-,
Means know-how. This is not the same

As practical wisdom, which means the self
Knowing when. As in, should one
When sitting nearly alone under a cinema dome?
The dialogue couch prompts, "Never, Sir,

When someone is watching." *(Enter a siren.)*
Now let's negotiate the question of the space
Between the two. And further, the issue

Of who decides which trumps—the trope of irony,
Or the trope of allegory? Each makes the picture of a perfect circle
Of pumpkin or pecan. Ergo, it's pi and it's Christmas.

And there's Paul, devout as ever,
On his way to a donkey-headed nowhere.

IN THE PRESENT AND PROBABLE FUTURE

Here we are viewing the land: waves of grave and grain.
That slight tremor? A house settling. A violent past walking through.

And over there, the burning deck. The political machine.
The inanimate come to life. The conventional flag wave.

Cormorants on pitched roofs watch the ship of state mandate folded
twice over. *Many ingenious lovely things are gone.* This turbulence. This

Coming one-two march through a landscape created.
The dark relative against the brilliance of the last act

Of some staged production. The cast bows. A tape player click, click,
Clicks. Some kind of clock. A unit of measurement.

We wish ourselves back on the boat. Wish for the answer
To the question: When should we walk out

Of the theater into the night? When should we accept that life is only
An exaggerated form of special pleading, romanticized

Beyond saying into moon, stone, flock and trees?
What in the picture would you get rid of? The land that stretches back

To prehistoric times? Myriad islands? Ice caps and etcetera?
The atmosphere? The human body? All of the above?

All but the latter? You'd like to keep human as an aspect of the formula
But rid it of its grappling ambition to destroy? Good luck with that.

What does it mean to have a point of view? What does it mean
To have a notable achievement? To succeed in representing

The nuances of a determinate activity?
Listen, however events turn out, if we want we can continue to see

The image of the moon as an outburst of lyric, a vision of John Keats
And his friends, but we still have the battle to fight.

How many more days will be there? The unperceptive will be busy
Believing in magic: crop circles, the unmanipulated image, definitions

That defy definition. Others will take at face value the less favorable
Consequences of both cynicism and commercialization.

The latter will say the flock is simply an assemblage,
An obsessive presence looking down on the building where someone sits

Predicting the landslide rate. Long after we are gone
We can say we were here. We were working, wittingly or not,

Towards the eventual erosion of places ground down
And fought over, especially in the literal sense—exploitation

And industrial damage. Nothing is lost. If anything, we gain
Experience. There will be that unsullied moment, down to the last

Detail, when the acquired interview and other quaint signs of demise
Will speak about us to the flood and the fire.

Q IS FOR THE QUICK

"The quick brown fox jumps
Over the lazy dog." It was a little bedtime story
And it was only told us if we would "be quiet."
But quiet was a difficult thing to be.
The heart makes a jump-start sound.

Each time someone comes up the steps
A foot gives off the white grate of shoe leather
As it meets a stair. They wanted us also to "be happy,"
Which was even more difficult
In view of the sad fact

That happiness is part of a pair called a "Smug Set"—
Happiness plus some other benignly self-satisfied state.
The story, once we "deserved" it, began,
"Shh, be quiet,"
Just as the quick baby was about to leap.

The story had various endings, each a variation
On the theme of danger that came from caution
Being thrown to the wind. Each ending was equally nefarious,
With the kit inevitably falling
Into the lazy dog's mouth—

The rust color of one, a fox, becoming one
With the cause of the other, a dog.
The idea of gore being nothing but a simple aside.
The endings were all perfect formulations, equal parts
Plaintive whine and equal parts plausible excuse.

R EQUALS THE ROYAL ROAD TO REALITY

Two dolls sit in a case,
Their unfeeling faces matching.
This, they say, is how one should look
At the world.

In another corner, Freud says yes
In the dark of primitive desire means yes
Forever. She puts down the book and thinks
About the forthcoming ordeal:

Washington on Nelson
Would cross the Washington Bridge.
Homer Simpson would be paired
With a blind man dragging a lyre.

There would be that card that said, THIS
IS THE WHAT YOU ARE LOOKING FOR.
The picture on the verso—an eye
And a notation on the edge

In minute type that said, "Here is the light."
Beside it, a hand-drawn lamp with no switch.
What do you want? Nothing.
And action in the form of a rabbit running,

Feet thumping in a patch of cabbage.
Then hiding in the watering can.
Its dull metal a dull bell as he taps one clawed paw
Against the floor, thinking, This

Is the nth deadline for doing.
Whatever I do now will be done.

REMINDS ME RAMONA

Twiddling our fingers at the frayed edge of the dance floor.
Our lady of forever. Our lawn ornament.
Now is the moment when she bows.

We have one wish and it's this: We live at the castle,
Read Kafka with a flashlight under the covers.
Stay steady on our feet.

Drink lemon iced-tea by the edge of the natatorium.
A plate-glass veranda,
A pool with a deep end ending in an alloy ladder,

Our brain case perpetually agape—a rubber band mass
About to unravel. And later,
We sit in black shadows and look out

On the red distances. The cast cauldron wall darkness passes.
Pour of dead blue air. The arrow flies into a furrow.
Morning melts the flakes.

And our mouthfuls grow to seas of foam, that white
To and from. To be something else.

SO, SO IT BEGINS MEANS IT BEGINS

And so it begins, Mickey, birthday cake (party), special
Night, whoops, and take a box.
So it begins, take a bow, hold your head up,
Scowl now. This is your own guitar.

Stop and see a movie.
Stop and see whether the eagle holds up at the end.
I'm leaving. See how I pull the door to.
The door is the floor and it's rising up,

Below is a dungeon. It's all you can see in the dark.
There is graffiti on the wall.
The bugle has ceded its call to power.
It's the time when we are waiting to be told.

Nothing is getting better. And nothing is getting worse.
A duck and a mouse. A house and a hat.
Having lunch and having a medal of honor.
Let's put our culture on a cartoon's.

Why not? Have the mouse answer the phone.
Have the receiver click. Then the real comes to
Its awful end. That point where, as he said, all came in
"With the shoutmost shoviality. Agog." Agog.

STILL AS IN A STILL AFTER STILL

How-then-why is charted like a map is a chart,
In four colors.
The typography forms another layer

That includes the map
Of the nap you took on Sunday.
The dream sky

That pressed in. A still is a picture
Of one segment. A tabletop rectangle
That is recommended. Okay, fine,

It was like that and like a de Chirico as well.
Sharp shadows. Summer sunlight.
An artichoke. A chokehold.

A multistory building
With layer after layer, each layer
Speaking like a person would say I wanted a cat,

I wanted a hat, I wanted to say happy something.
It was like a tree trunk
Formed from a handful of ashes

In a dark forest. In the dream you're looking
Into a light like the type that used to shine down
On a suspect in a movie not made anymore

So much more exact are the tactics
For forcing a speech.
Through the light comes a sound,

A roundness and depth of a fire truck cutting its way
Through a crowd of cars halted for fear.
There is a house that's off-camera

In flames. A contrasting white ice cap melts
In the corner at the camera angle.
Every four inches, fear already fallen,

And in the air more,
The color of fire flowing down branches.

T EQUALS TIME TO BE TAMED

The rain made the street darker
In the late afternoon. I made a snake
Wrap itself around a stack of green paper.
The money disappeared.

The sun came out and added shadow,
Inside of which, the figment of a life.
And inside that, the feeling in a fragment.
["Wherefore, villain, hast thou failed?"

(*Sister Carrie*, Theodore Dreiser)]
All the while, an extravagant wonder
Was ending the way it began: in wonder.
To our right, the inhabitants of an ant farm

Were exiting a cracked glass
In the slow mode. An art form
Made from the hinge of day,
And the wheel of night.

A hard ball came through the shield
Of the window and landed in a lap.
Egg of leisure. Leaves of grass. Tara tomorrow.
A feminine face of defiance can be made

Pretty by makeup and utter hyperbole.
The action occurring before the eyes
Could be shot to the back of the brain.
Ergo, a movie just for you.

Suddenly, there's a tin man walking a dog.
"Goodnight, goodnight."
"Goodnight, government."
The sharks are circling so we say

It's all too much and yet
We choose to continue the fluid trend
Toward slipping and stopping
While continuing the greed

For the seen and the voice-over said.
"Goodnight." Kiss and kiss-kiss.
The near-silver night goes on. In the dark,
The artichoke watches the train from the window,

While it waits for the drama of morning.
While it waits for time to mean more than a store,
Which is also called waiting in vain.

There it was, the half-moon.
The almost half-moon.
The stupid moon.
There it was. The night surrounding the day.
The stupid night. The stupid day.
The day had been hot.
The day had been a biography:
The thief, the convict, the traitor.
There you were: the thief.
One afternoon when you were nine.
It could have been June. Now you're here.
You and the moon. You and the endless night.
You, with the stupidity of the moon.
The haze at the inner edge.
Russia sinking into the sea.
The Antarctic sinking. The permafrost melting.
How dare the moon sit in the sky
Looking like half of itself.
Close your eyes and sing the song
Of the closed eyes. Close your eyes and don't sing.
But sink at the deep edge
Of the pool. This is the what,
The wherefore, the why. Why die?
For this. This sinking into. This end.
What thefts aren't shallow and small?

U IS FOR UNITED

The contrast with liberty is striking: impediment,
Impediment, impediment.
What sort of guarantee is that?
My x-ray heart, stark against the light box
Of servitude. The claim of the so-called Crown

An unarguable flat-hand stratagem of force.
The blunt multitude—a mouthful
Of nail heads—requires empowerment.
Someone comes forward from the shadow
Behind the drape into a scrape of light and says,
"Look," and we see the nightly news:

"Here we are, David, standing in front of a landslide."
"What does it look like, Chet?"
"It looks like a landslide."
"Thank you for that."

Our thoughts imprisoned by the image,
A monstrous hectoring narrative,
Relieved only by the unflattering
Bodice of the newscaster, pearls on her earlobes.
(Those were the pearls that were her eyes.)

Behind her, a stoical rubble of rock.
I believe you know there is, on the one hand,
The concept of putting up. And on the other,
The concept of skepticism. The latter demanding
Action. May I please have a short-term loan

Of agate to build a house against thunder and thirst.
Yes, I know, the gold star is tarnished in the cap
On the coffin lid. An oil-spill iridescence

Catches the dying light. "Sorry," says Cerberus,
Each mouth moving in unison.

V IS THE DIVER

V, the diver, goes down and up again,
According to a beat
Kept by a personal pencil-point director.
"You, over there." V points to "you" and you,
Never objective, look vacantly away.

V is for victory and verisimilitude.
Roy is a ventriloquist.
He has a Jerry Mahoney doll.
Its head lolls and it pants as it asks,
"Isn't it hot in here?" Roy says, no, it's not.

At least not so very.
Complaining, Roy says, is a vice.
There's a V that defines the lip of the girl
Over there with a lovely vulnerable canted body.
One hip juts out, just slightly, thoughtlessly.

Nothing annuls this moment and yet
It's not the body
But the ingenious scheming interior
That one connects with as it unfurls its nonverbal wish
To be one, let alone, and two, act

In an allegory of the hidden within,
Or, if not that, then three, be
A symbol of the eternal grand ineffable.
The ghost is one with the living person, no?
Along with the embarrassment of being

A vista, in which the confirming detail is thought
To communicate the whole,
There is the very thing
One doesn't like to think:
That this lovely may be meant as tomorrow's

Blood-spattered head married to a headline
And observed through the morning's View-Master.
The voltmeter measures the moment
While a voice one associates with a voluptuous life
Continues to throw itself up

To the stage from the bar area in back.
There's little to do during this period of hectoring
But wait with due vigilance
For the vibraphone to start up again. For Roy
To resume. Afterwards, we let our feet hang over

The edge of the vacuous and dangle in the void
While we watch in fear our own faces
Go strange in the windows.
The houselights are on dim
And most of us agree,

That to varying degrees, we felt something
During the lull—little sorrows
That are virtually unnamable, yet so profound
They are sometimes perceived as visceral.
It was like getting lost, someone says,

In a vortex. Another says, "I remembered
To breathe." Meanwhile, against the night sky, V
Is again on the high dive. It's a repeat
Of the first full moon of the last summer solstice.
The elation we feel is equal only to our angst.

W IS FOR WHATEVER

"Ally Ally In Come Free" is heard
In the evening breeze, and then,
"The camel draws the hearse,
The camel draws the hearse,

Hi-ho the derry-o
The camel draws the hearse."
It's René Clair speaking clearly, saying,
Even death is a joke when it's spoken.

And what is left but the crossword puzzle
That replaces "one" with "1"
And condenses the answers to something
One has to think about. That morning, that is.

She put down the paper
And walked over to the back door.
She looked out on Eden.
She thought she could see the snake

Wrapped around a rusted tree.
And there, too, was the persistent mud puddle
From which a stray dog was drinking.
His pale pink tongue lapping

At the surface of what was wet. She saw how
The mythology of blackness and strangeness
Combined in the drinking dog.
Overlapped. His coat cloaked

The same network underneath (red blood
And blue venous return) as royalty
Or anyone. And in that way,
There was nothing new.

Time was still Death's other. She knew,
What was waiting: a serpentine mosaic
In which the era ends
By virtue of a back-and-forth motion

Of an eraser. And everyday,
The morning mirror
Was a photo-booth miniature mirror.
Wakefulness sensing, the way

Machines can, that this was the moment
To become again. The flash of the sun,
The snake and the dog,
All panning the face. Making it so.

THE WAKE WAS A LINE AND WE WATCHED

While we stood in the window and wept.
Well, not wept but sniveled
A little and wiped our eyes
On a coat sleeve. What

Were we thinking, I wonder now.
It was fall.
It was clear. A boat sat
Throwing a reflection of itself

Onto a body of water.
It sits and sits. As the ornament is
A monument so is the bird in the sky
One with the eyes

That were taking it all in.
An argument for a theory
Of all-in-oneness. All as all. Imagine
The "I" as a camera turned on

To a mirror.
Where the face in the mirror
Isn't that of the one looking in
But of Jacqueline Onassis

Or someone else famous
Beyond saying.
A full fifteen minutes.
It's in the nature of looking

At the future while married to the moment.
It's Disney's "Mickey
And The Broken Mirror Mishap"
All over again.

The jagged glass reforming
Into a narrative where
The core event keeps clicking into place
As a great, a terrible, shattering.

This thought leads straight
To the darkest thought: I miss home.
Like a child misses home, or
A line drawing of a Quebec Marmot.

That's what happens.
Meanwhile, the madness.
The brain-gray concourse.
The utter factuality of the few true things.

X EQUALS THE PLACE WHERE WE ARE

A ball bowled along the ground
In the game of cricket is called a daisy cutter.
It makes sense. A girl and a coin:
On one side of the gold piece
There's a crown and on the other
Side there's a symbol signifying a day
After the fair, i.e., the fair you came to see
Is over. In otherwise, you are too late
(Fat raindrops morph
Into bloated close-up acetate tears.
The movie is X minutes from over)
To catch fate's arrow as it leaves
The anachronistic bow (diagram ink-printed
On vellum and then some). And then,
When life is over one is "gone
To the place of safekeeping,
Where duffy Jonah was sent to."
Where Davy Jones is Jonah.
Everything is always changing. And yet,
Here we are, you and I, us,
Upstairs, two flights of stairs to get there,
Out of the wave of water,
In the flooded postal service's dead-letter office.
Don't you love it here?
A bench of deep green leatherette, swirl pattern
Without dent or ding,
With a bent chrome bedrock
That invites us to sit. But instead, we're stretched out
On the floor, unable to go any lower.
We are at what is called dead-lift.
At the exhumation,
The weight of the box resists gravity.
We pull but it drags
Us down with it. We go in the house

Where we don't quite belong,
Where the shutters are drawn. We stutter,
"We don't quite belong here."
"O dio mio" becomes "O Dear Me."
In between is "Or ever I had seen that day, Horatio."
She had once read a story where two knights die
While kissing the hand of someone
Else's wife. What did the wife have on her hand?
"Till death us do part," in body ink.
Dénouer, to untie. To untangle the plot
Threads, which is to say, the denouement
Of the story concerning some group
Of denizen naturalized by the daisy cutter
As it rolls along the ground,
Making a path in the Blutgang grass.
The blunt sword carried by a king
At coronation is also called a cutter
And is meant to mean mercy.
"Let me not be a troglodyte.
Let me know how to read the world
Through a shim of blindness."
(The king, behind a curtain, is heard begging
For all of us.) But then there is fate, again,
In the form of a door and someone
Or something comes through.
And when they do, the oncoming object becomes
A rolling cog in a video camcorder, an egg-roll zoom lens
Filming a girl in a camisole
With beautiful flame-red hair. "Rita, is that you?
We're taking you home now, Darling.
Close your vermilion satin dressing gown
And put on your Excellent Red lip gloss."
And out you go to a black anachronistic car

Where a black box lies on the back seat. Pandora's.
Lock the door. All past is gone.
In the jelly cellar and in the carport
Under that cedar shingle roof—the tract house
Ranch-style, with a Danish-teak mid-century-modern interior.
A pine tree shedding needles. Gone and over.
The egg of the eye turns back
Into the socket for such a small moment,
But long enough to denote contempt, or relief. Or death.
Sure. That's the omen indicating there will be an end.
The daisies mowed over. Someday. Or tomorrow.
As in, "Tomorrow is another," or
"Tomorrow, tomorrow, tomorrow, O Horatio."
Meanwhile, that girl with the coin is lying
In the grass but inside her head,
The mirrored walls with every face she ever made,
And the blinding chrome of the spanking machine.

Y IS FOR YEAR'S MIND

All the O's, those of silence and those of absence,
Refused to mention who
Made all those missteps, leading to the edge of the edge

And over. Listen: Two have been left behind
On the stage and are still
Speaking. One is saying, "You know

I love you." The other is listening. It's a rerun
Of the HBO show, *Six Feet Under.*
There is a window in the room.

There are flowers in bloom.
The Eames chair in the entryway is empty.
There's a pair of scissors. She is trimming her hair,

Leaving today's wisps in the sink that's tomorrow's.
She changes, leaving
Today on the floor. Looking in from the door:

The bed is red and yellow. Streetlight leaks
In around the pulled window shades.
Light leaks between the two days that make up before

And after. She falls asleep. There is wreckage.
There is reiteration.

Z IS FOR ZED AT THE END

After the 0 but before the over,
There's hope. And then there is none.
There are simply the sheets
Which cover the waiting world. There are the seats
From which we watch. And hover.

At the wedding of now and be ever, someone makes note
That the Mickey Mouse clock on the mantel is stuck
And still. Someone else adds, "May there never be a snake."
And another says, "And never a poison apple."
Once we gave the apple and tree a story.

Once we let the snake speak. In a whisper, it said,
"Let no one fall." And then laughed
Into its tail. And wasn't it Eve who is said to have said, "Hello"?
And, "You're right, this is quite tasty."
All the while, on the opposite page, Ophelia

In her small lake. Ophelia, the water—
Edging her blue-tinged lips and bloated face—
The color of tin. The evening's hair all laced with lily.
A hint of Madonna.
A face. A bed ready. A bed made.

Z STANDS FOR ZERO HOUR

The mind soothing itself. Creating a static buzz,
In other words a hum, as sleep kicks in.
"Knowledge originates from direct experience."

Mao Zedong's face faces out
From the gallery wall. The news is this:
Between now and now is a rest. A mirror

Where the walker you saw in the window disappears.
It's called opacity. Which is evidence
That Mao is gone. The gang of four is gone.

The door is closed. The evening falls
Into the outline. Tree branch, tiny lights
Wrapping the tree trunk. The idea of winter, a season

Or two away. In here, it's quiet.
The suit is folded and tucked into a tissue-lined box.
The box is polka-dotted. Time-like layers

Of the sheerest substance stacked one atop the other
And finally forming a substrate
Never quite solidifying but after the fact forming a z

With air between the horizontals.
With air in each alveoli.
With air surrounding outside and in. Nothing is free.

PART II

Venice and Thomas Mann. In the movie you actually see the mascara form-
ing a toxic slick. Dripping down his face. Afterwards, the lacerating realiza-
tion. Your own tragic edge of a rug and looking. Mother in the immediate
distance. The next room. Across this room. An ever-present eye. Watching
but not acting. Lost. The ash of us against the wall and on the floor. A gray
line. I didn't have an imagination. I can't imagine where we are going. The
difference? None. How did one know what to call a thing? No one cared.
I was standing with two boys. A gravel road that led to other trailers. An
afternoon. Or a morning. One boy's name is Wally. The other boy is lower
class. My mother doesn't like his mother. Wally is more refined. I could see
it. Even then. Four? He's the one to want. I had the idea (urge, compulsion).
To kiss him. And why? Who was I imitating? There's no way to recapture
that. The boy goes home. He is still going.

You just go on. You kiss him and for a portion of a what? A second? You
expect something. You have no doubt. You've seen this somewhere and you
know he will like what he gets this. He will be reconstructed to belong to
you. Like what? I don't know. Just instinct. I do. Did. In the moment and
then. The stun of having done. First awareness of thought as desire I know
nothing of that happens. The not good that looks on while the boy's face
breaks and draws into itself and out of the gaping mouth with a glistening
curled lower lip a sound. Loud and coarse extravagant wail. Trails him as
he runs he to his trailer. His tin can full of tables and chairs and beds. A
shelf of whatnot.

The worst kind of astonishment. The irrefutable knowledge that he would
be never now. Moreover, the certain expectation of punishment. His mother
knocking hard on our door. Brought out before her in the dead zero of
humiliation, a target at the center so horrific I begin to wait with want-
ing. Just to get it over. I imagine. It never comes. I am in that state forever.
Second by second. Every subsequent occasion of erring. Everything slights
me. I see it.

A feeling I would be exposed. It stayed in my mind as a central element. The stage. The silver screen. Profound and pervasive coloring. At a distance from myself. I was born and raised to be set in relief. What I wanted to say is that everything has its opposite side. Not being a person but a character on stage. Authorial impersonality. Another fact. An illness. It affected everything. Reinforcing what was already there. Reinforcing I not being the self. Memory hemorrhaging. Self loss. An element. A life shaped. Beginning. Middle. End. That clichéd belief. It would be a surgeon to my own demise. A classical adolescent trope. Customary. But despite myself I was. Longer. What else could I do. Plastic and its opposite. Impenetrable and unchanging. Unchangingly mysterious.

Christmas aluminum tree. A beige wool loathing of prudence. A web of prudence. Stuck in the adhesion. From there, a window onto aphasia. An aftermath of great fatigue. A comedy of errors is a tragedy. Denial at war with prudence. I am not. Going. Nameless malady. Match-girl melody glass looking in on the impossible. Later, migraines, scarlet fever, mercury fillings, dysphoria as the opposite of euphoria. The synaptic clefts. Gray. Draconian. Firmly imaginative. Gilt working as a mimic. Mother. Her head. My head. Hide your life. Impersonality and touch. Only that made me real. Delirium of fever. The car ride ("Let's go for a ride!") as consolation for what? The impossible. The sadness exacerbated by a single string of assaults. Fear and precarious field of vision. I will not. I will not. Do I make myself clear? An illness of memory and imagination escaping. Fireworks heard and not seen. The fear of a spark. Terror that death would alter not me but my mother.

I was left alone except for work and breathing. And books. My sister. My older characterological opposite. Disappointed only when the television screen was smaller than expected. The house a dugout and not a mansion. I had none. I didn't know what was in me. Simon Lagree. The perfect description for what we felt. Had I read the book? What does anyone inherit? I didn't know how I knew. Terror of not. A steady state punctuated by knowledge I didn't know. Neurotic relative to a snarled Kafkaesque un-doneness. No warm anticipation. That wouldn't be dampened. Like my sister but with a different conclusion. Every day would be the same. Waking on the dot to that repeated realization. The crosshairs of a hidden life. An echo of a before. Before what? Before a lifelong self-censure the moment anyone offered two inseparables.

The hallucinated moment when two were one. Kindness and touch as one before resuming the stupefying disappointment. Defenseless against the external world. Mortal danger. Terrified of losing yet wanting the apparent opposite, losing the self instead of the other. An ordeal. My sister undaunted. Her boyish in her blue dress with puff sleeves. Me in pink. Roses. Mystery of my sister. The splendid genius of distance. The most proximate candidate for affection. Downcast. The mother a spinning top whose painted stripes cannot be touched or teased apart into true colors. Who are *you* (the caterpillar to Alice)? A hidden life. Mother of nothing. I look like her. Everyone says so. Comparison always happens at arm's length. Discrete. More obsessed by necessity. Extraordinary. Beautiful. A love of beautiful clothes but having after a certain date, none but necessity. An erosion of the true self. Inept and protective. Opposites. Afraid of losing her children as she lost her. Where did she keep those? They would hemorrhage from time to time. Then we would see the blood of the orphanage. The rats under the bed. The discomfort. Tell me a story. The story is always discomfort. The sense that this would be no model of expansiveness. Built-in distance. "Little lambs eat ivy," she would say. Her voice sounded.

Houndstooth check with a canine incisor on every corner. Finally, I am not myself. "All the reasons," a woman says, using her hands to shape an orb. So, completion is an orb that implies the abbreviated narrative? The gone world. The center of emptiness. Forever means since I don't know how old I am. I hear a song. People say, "I don't know" when talking about the self's knowledge. They don't mean what I mean. These actual events coming back as if actual. The architecture of preoccupation. That doesn't mean I can enter the spiral Guggenheim rotunda with walls filled with packets of fragments. Small and large and images. A transfiguration of the idea of time. The surface marred. I'm tied. I mean tired. I think it is a fault. I sleep enough.

It's a movie. It's 1996. The one where one sociopath puts another in a woodchipper. Blood makes a mess of the white snow. The ransomed woman dies, the father-in-law dies, one sociopath dies, two casual witnesses die. More dead but I don't remember. I took the subway with an axe in the back of my head. That is to say the brutality. I come up out of the subway. I cross the street. A horn doesn't stop behind me. I cross and I cross. On the other side I look back to see the commotion. The driver of the car looks at me, the horn still not stopping, meets my eyes. He sees into me and says, "Not you, fuck-face." Twelve years later I'm a frayed edge. I'm under everything I know.

The secondary characters. The stepfather's children. A train. A mother in Baltimore who put them on it when she hears he has remarried. My mother said so. Stunned. They didn't stay long. A summer maybe. I don't know. I remember my mother's face. "I can't stand liars. If there's anything I can't stand, it's a liar. I can't stand Kenny." I don't mind him. More than the summer because my sister has a memory. Sonny misspelled Wednesday and was made to wear a dress. Hers. Weakness. Woman. I don't know except what I hear. I don't hear this. Or if I do. I don't want it to stand in the way of something good that I don't often see. Something. He was sent away by my mother. Now. He goes.

My brain takes the shape of a Smith-Corona hulk. A letter in the center. He disappeared. His two sons arrived with lost expressions. My mother. Their mother. Put them on a train from Baltimore and then called. Was I in the train? Was I in the car? Watching what? Seeing what? Long lines of train cars rust colored or silver windowed. There is something thrilling. There is something transient. Colored eggs. Marshmallow candy in clear plastic. Baskets retrieved from a closet shelf. Cellophane green grass. The waxy chocolate rabbit's hollow head gone. Munchkins singing in their cut-down clothes. Which old witch? The wicked. "Who put that there?" when there didn't exist. It was a trick the late mind plays. The hallucination of something to fill the emptiness. Pointing. The pathos now that the actor is dead. Ding dong the witch. "All the reasons," she says, using her hands to shape the shape. As if completion's all were an orb. The abbreviated narrative. That's all. I move on.

My aunt arrives. She has a boyfriend. Who says after my mother and aunt and sister leave to go somewhere together. He says. And I'm left with him. I'm six. He says do you want to go sit in my car. I never say. We sit side by side on the seat. I look at the dash. I leave myself somewhere else. It seems only a second. Then they are back. From wherever they went. His hand is opening the car door and my mother or is it my aunt says what are you doing and I wonder what he will say. Nothing or something. Like, we was just sitting in the car. No one says anything. We all go inside.

The baby gave us a bottle brush and we. We did the dishes. We played soda shop with soapsuds. Reach and a plate breaks. Its form now two from one in the bottom of the ironing basket. It never empties. It forgets itself. Until one day. The emphatic reduction of don't. The reiteration. The recommendation. Be good. The sweater of the seventh year. The white trim. Fake pearls shedding their thin skin. Fibers resting as molecules of basement when the tornado was warned. The casserole dish on the table. The neighbor children's pale faces. The neighbor woman as tall as a father.

The lamp on the sill in the bedroom topples. To wash. The windows. Out of that emptiness, the lamp falls. The bulb breaks. And now a scar. Okay, a car. A car and the door not completely closed so. My brother's head out the window and hanging on and I am next. The baby must be my mother's. The door opens and he is hanging. The horror now takes shape. Yesterday was long. Sitting on the steps. The black dog named Cocoa. The neighbors. The nights. The huge capsule-shaped gas container. My mother afraid the hot day will make the gas explode. She rinses it with hose water. Every day my stepfather on the side of the hill. The shotgun. Rats in the ashes of the burned garbage. The flattened cans. A creamed-corn label singed. There are rabbits in a cage. We feed them. We eat them.

In the dark of the Savoy, the screen. The stick of the shoe on the floor. The line outside the in. The sister. Once my mother stood in the back just inside the door that closed out the world. Leaving is left. The tomato-soup trestle the car goes under. The eyes deriding whatever pleasure you had is taken from you. Yes. I move on. Go.

You're becoming boiling water. You're wading in, your cap snug on your frantic head. Your feet perhaps mired in maybe. In the beginning or end of an error. The weight of the drape that's covering you is the weight of white in the middle of March. Behind your eyes, black shoe warped. A squall is formed by the uneven list of answers to questions about serving as a volunteer for a year. That is punctuated by the thought of someone mannered and polished, but morally bankrupt. However, what was the goal? To create the play of light across a sculpture of World War I? No. "I hardly need to abstract things, for each object is unreal enough." The fraternal tone of the experimenter, "Are you comfortable in there?" The ruins strewn. Strewn with what? What will you see? A grandiose spectacle of water bubbling. That there is no better cause, is the negative reply. And you, clean as a white cap on the bottom.

LIKE IS LIKE

Nights were spent in a parlor of darkness that had two windows, one for looking out at a tangled mass composed of reminders of what had or hadn't been done that day, and the second for looking out on changing faces that represented past moments.

"Fine," someone said, "put on the white dress." "If that's what you want."

Who was he but a painter known for his paintings? Portraits of women and children posed like statues. Most famous of all, the *Bride and Marriage* early work, with bold brushstrokes and white veil, flowers and a long twentieth century.

A dog rushes after a man with miserable coordination. He stumbles and falls down. The man looks like someone who knows that's how it goes. Now she's out of the car, standing on her head or walking on her hands. Someone says, "Look at you."

Start in the middle at the point where the accused stands, the headline titles are already set, and nature is only a stage away. Let's admit we can rely on constancy occasionally. Just not very often. And now, reduce that idea to matter, and what do you get? A knockabout exchange where thought is trying and failing, blustering, and casting about. And remember the accused. He's dear to us. We worshipped him. He was the simile for the grand everything. This is the appeal of the figure. The subject who stands in the pictorial field, his relations standing by as marks on a wall. Everything is unpredictable. And that's the only thing of interest. Think how fierce a "grimace" is. It works.

For a long time now.... That was how the story began, there was a buildup of "for this sake" "for that." There was a stairway. And sensation. Condensation, compression, a solid body becoming no wider than an exception.

What do we really know? Roughly that we are looking through the crook of our own arm and we have a commitment to keep. We can't keep saying that's just the way it is. We could cross our legs. We could nod our collective and singular head. But for how much longer? For as long as the decision stays unresolved. It's ostensible stasis. Who speaks like that? Standing partly in and partly out of the picture: two officers, one on either side. The walls are a muffled green, as cliché as a delicate face on a female body. He killed her. That's what we believe. But our eye sockets weren't there. To feel smug is so marvelous. This strikes me as a real danger. The kind of danger that is not so much pretty as prettified because it's not ugly and it's not grotesque. Negation is the form of oneself, minus the fear. True enough. Every trial is a trial of social strength. Of the grandeur of protest on the grounds of the quarrel.

The accused has an interesting silhouette. Maybe even a distinction. Say we want to paint his picture. But we don't know how to paint. We only know draw, harm, and indicate. So, still, that gives an impression. Or take someone vestigial to the plot. Take the one who keeps his or her distance. She is propped against a wall, or leaning in the opposite direction of a half of a single plate. Is she moving toward the broken piece that may have fallen to the floor? Or is she slouching away from the work of cleaning the counter?

The accused is the worst of the well behaved. He has remade his own representation. That was never his goal but he's done it. Or perhaps he declares that it was. That, to us, is so unpalatable. To want to be what the brutal have said that you are. What a hopelessly clotted wrong. We shudder. Or turn. This is to be anticipated. The truculent aftershocks. The maximal visual information is the canvas, or the newsprint, or the not-seeable. It's not so much a scale as a checkerboard. At the top of the hill is an illusion. It arises from little sloping shadows. This organizes the whole scene. The fixed reality of pure emptiness. It will hardly matter, the conjured. The accused has his struggles. He has a reprieve. Two years follow. His unpreparedness also has the shape of a grid. The wavering month does too. The main doubts. The mental depictions. No one objects too strenuously at this point. Trying to make sense is really a device. Every bit as much a sign of proximity as anything else. The paradox goes deeper. It goes to the fact that the whereabouts of the original are unknown.

Take for example Flaubert's idea that "c'est moi." She is me but she is also she. And now what do we know? There is a possible "organic intensity," a word that comes with its own old manifesto. It's terrifying to see how quickly oil moves to aluminum. We are always the child. Looking at the spattered scenario. The world a void against an environment. The accused steadily goes from point to point. What does it mean to be well-adjusted? What does it mean to tell about the search for an event that will include the act of accusation against the right party by one not connected to the event? Or, let's honor the percentage of failure. I don't know whether the accused is guilty. I know there are unconscious illusions. The double take that looks back at the decline. On second thought, the profile is a little formulaic. In at the eyes, out at the nose. Lips. A chin.

In this case, we have to handle him differently. It may depend on the rightly held belief in "began again, and so on." A transparent wall, hardwood floors, stuff. Someone saying they have a feeling that rises and falls. Nature never grimaces. That's an explicit duality. As clunky as it is. It's April. Yes, the accused has evaded the issue of what he prefers but he's also been declared someone to be pushed back against the wall. He's a jawline. Somewhere between general and regular. We are between massive and faceted. We are resting in the green shadows of the eye socket. It's the end of the day. We see the upper lip. Someone is speaking to someone else across a gap. The conversation seems staged. That's crucial.

The exception was a snowstorm in the form of five boxes of minutia, each equal to the soothing time of walking the drive to and from the stretch of absence between the first and the final occasion, spooning applesauce into the fracture of a face that was a slack mouth and the grave, as it were. A particular Kabuki mask atop a specific hush never heard otherwise. The scent of lily, the sight of a train car fallen from the track and down on its side. What sort of crane or mechanical force would be needed to right it? She would. What? She rubs soap on her face. And everything. Keep your little "tarp" shut. That lacerating miniature. An echo of some little mirror forced forward over invisible wires. Had someone gotten herself "in trouble"? She and two other girls went to smoke a pack of Benson & Hedges, the green and gold hard-pack. And now the sound of canned laughter in her inner ear. On a front page was a picture in the paper. Rectangular reproduction ink blots of frontal views and facile gestures of a life now reduced to the bus rolled twice down the steep embankment before it burst into fame.

The steady noise of a one two. A measure. An ergo. Just the daily kind. The adequate distraction from whatever multiple minor concerns were ever present. The unturned knob. The phone. Daily darkness although technically it's no longer. An absence or a presence. The object of tragedy when tragedy has agency and rings the phone. The day isn't a gray-dressed interval. So there is a heroic figure in some formless shadow of a dream? The face of Freud imbedded in the moving silver. She watches it from the corner while standing against a wall.

They were walking to watch a free film. After the dorm room lysergic acid had melted. She said, "Is the sky really that color?" A tug on the shirtsleeve of a steady pace. They were near. Could he hear? Could he speak? "Is the sky really that color?" He looked directly at her as if a stranger were asking him *something*. He took an unarguable tone, "The sky is whatever color you think it is." Who could counter that one has one's own perceptions, however nicely skewed they were for the necessary pretense for communication was gone. How could he know what she was seeing?

The dust rises off the attire of an age. An engraved rattle in a vitrine. A moment eased from a "Come here." Her mother is at her post. She reluctantly closes, assumes her place at the side of the glass-fronted cupboard. The costume jewelry. Her black jet broach. Deco flat expanse broken by a rhinestone studded chrome strip that crosses in a diagonal. She stands tip-toe to see. Too much what, she wonders? Money? Should she let it go? Of course she should. And she does when her mother says, "I don't know why."

Egg dotted with tan and taupe like the edge of each side of the rectangle where the oak and the acorns were underfoot. The shattered weave of light between leaves when looked up from under. Systematic swish of chemicals across the synapses. Inside the braincase, "Do you want?" No. Shakes her head. Nothing but what there is.

A feeling of mild lovely but lost. Ancient Greek cannot be completely reconciled with present day English. The belief in a text is tangential to faith. Hard-wiring is still within sight. A cabinet length is the distance delivered by chance. The preordained limit. As if—Is this? Says, "Remember that a snow scene can turn into an enormous fruitcake tin." A yo-yo pulling away and being tugged to what can be known. A smile for the boy who has a loan that comes due every second Tuesday. The hall closet filled with books with spines facing outward and forming a readable text of titles that merged together to pose questions about the status quo. "I guess" was all she ever answered. And something he said.

Notes

The quotations in "ABC Plus E: Cosmic Aloneness Is the Bride of Existence" are taken from a chapter entitled "Adventures Among the Existentialists" in Michael Scammell's *Koestler: The Literary and Political Odyssey of a Twentieth-Century Skeptic*. Thanks to Michael Scammell for their use. "For I seem dying, as one going in the dark / To fight a giant" is taken from Browning's "Pauline, a Fragment of a Confession." The first five stanzas of "E Is Everywhere" owe a debt to (and borrow language from) an online posting by Stewart Clarke on October 14, 1998, on the Sylvia Plath Forum (www.sylviaplathforum.com/bees.html). "Sheep in fog," in "The Electric Eventual," is the title of a poem by Sylvia Plath. In "J Is for Jammed, as in Stuck" the quotation "I hardly need to abstract things, for each object is unreal enough" is by Max Beckmann, taken from his 1938 lecture, "On My Painting." "Riveted to some detail of the desert" in "Just Seen, Just Said" is from *Ill Seen, Ill Said*. The title of "In the Present and Probable Future" comes from a subtitle in Alexis de Tocqueville's *Democracy in America*, "The Present and Probable Future Condition of the Three Races That Inhabit the Territory of the United States." "Many ingenious lovely things are gone" in the same poem is from Yeats's "Nineteen Hundred and Nineteen." The quotation "With the shoutmost shoviality. Agog" in "So, So It Begins Means It Begins" is taken from *Finnegans Wake*. "All genuine knowledge originates from direct experience" in "Z Stands for Zero Hour" is by Mao Zedong.

Acknowledgments

Thanks to the editors of the following journals and anthologies where these poems, sometimes in earlier versions, were published:

The Agriculture Reader: "Heretofore Having in Mind," "B Is for Beckett," "I in a War," and "Z Stands for Zero Hour"; *Bat City Review:* "Her in the Eye of a Hurricane" and "T Equals Time to Be Tamed"; *Black Warrior Review:* "H Is Here Is a Song, Now Sing" and "W Is for Whatever"; *Boulevard:* "Just Seen, Just Said" and "O Is in Outside"; *Boston Review:* "E Is Everywhere"; *Conjunctions:* "Death and Disappearance" and "N as in Nevermore"; *Court Green:* "Reminds Me Ramona"; *Denver Quarterly:* "G Is Going," "J Is for Jammed, as in Stuck," and "Like Is Like"; *Electronic Poetry Review:* "F Is for Forgetting" and "Ghosts and Grays"; *The Emily Dickinson Journal:* "The Electric Eventual" (as "E Is for Emily"); *Filter:* "Heretofore Having in Mind"; *Gulf Coast:* "K as in F Blank Blank K" and "Z Is for Zed at the End"; *The Kenyon Review:* "V Is the Diver" and "The Wake Was a Line and We Watched"; *LIT:* "U Is for United" and "Unknown and Unknowable"; *The New Republic:* "D Is Dying, as One Going in the Dark"; *The New Yorker:* "Beast Brutality" and "So, So It Begins Means It Begins"; *The New York Times:* "The Present and Probable Future"; *The Paris Review:* "Mystery at Manor Close" and "Q Is for the Quick"; *Poetry:* "ABC Plus E: Cosmic Aloneness Is the Bride of Existence," "And as in Alice," and "L Equals Look"; *A Public Space:* "Outnumbered at 0" and "A Equals All of a Sudden"; *River Styx:* "Y Is for Year's Mind"; *Salt:* "For Freud," "M as in Masks," "Night after Night," "O Means the Mouth," "Twenty to June," and "X Equals the Place Where We Are"; *Southwest Review:* "C is for Cher"; *Tin House:* "Magic Makes Everything Right," "For the Final Report," and "Consider This Corruption"; *Tusculum Review:* "R Equals the Royal Road to Reality"; *The Walrus* (Canada): "I as in Justice."

"P Equals Pie" and "Mystery at Manor Close" appeared in *American Hybrid: A Norton Anthology of New Poetry,* eds. Cole Swensen and David St. John (New York: W. W. Norton, 2009).

"And as in Alice" appeared in the *Alhambra Poetry Calendar 2008*, "F Is for Forgetting" in the *Alhambra Poetry Calendar 2009*, "C Is for Cher" in the *Alhambra Poetry Calendar 2010*, ed. Shafiq Naz (Bertem, Belgium: Alhambra Publishing).

"B Is for Beckett" was printed as a broadside by the Bow & Arrow Press at Harvard University.

Thanks to my friends, especially Mónica de la Torre and Timothy Donnelly. And to Eleanor Sarasohn, whose invaluable comments helped shape this manuscript. And to Bill Clegg. And to Rusty Bang. Thanks to David Levinthal for the use of his photograph, *Café*, for the cover. Also to the Rockefeller Foundation for a residency at the Bellagio Study Center where some of these poems were written. And to the Bogliasco Foundation for a residency at the Liguria Study Center where others were written.

"C Is for Cher" is for Bin Ramke
"Her in the Eye of a Hurricane" is for Eleanor Sarasohn
"I in a War" is for Anna Rabinowitz
"P Equals Pie" is for Jon Cook

Mary Jo Bang is the author of five previous poetry collections, including *Elegy,* winner of the 2007 National Book Critics Circle Award in Poetry and a *New York Times* Notable Book. She has received a fellowship from the Guggenheim Foundation, a Hodder Fellowship from Princeton University, and has twice won the Alice Fay di Castagnola Award from the Poetry Society of America. She lives in Saint Louis, Missouri, where she is a professor of English and teaches in the creative writing program at Washington University.

This book was designed by Rachel Holscher. It is set in Adobe Caslon Pro type by BookMobile Design and Publishing Services, and manufactured by Friesens on acid-free paper.